RECONSTRUCTION

AND THE RENEWAL OF LIFE

T0346133

RECONSTRUCTION

AND THE RENEWAL OF LIFE

THREE LAY SERMONS

BY

W. R. SORLEY

KNIGHTBRIDGE PROFESSOR OF MORAL PHILOSOPHY
FELLOW OF KING'S COLLEGE, CAMBRIDGE
AND OF THE BRITISH ACADEMY

CAMBRIDGE
AT THE UNIVERSITY PRESS
1919

CAMBRIDGE UNIVERSITY PRESS
Cambridge, New York, Melbourne, Madrid, Cape Town,
Singapore, São Paulo, Delhi, Mexico City

Cambridge University Press
The Edinburgh Building, Cambridge CB2 8RU, UK

Published in the United States of America by Cambridge University Press, New York

www.cambridge.org
Information on this title: www.cambridge.org/9781107629264

© Cambridge University Press 1919

This publication is in copyright. Subject to statutory exception
and to the provisions of relevant collective licensing agreements,
no reproduction of any part may take place without the written
permission of Cambridge University Press.

First published 1919
First paperback edition 2013

A catalogue record for this publication is available from the British Library

ISBN 978-1-107-62926-4 Paperback

Cambridge University Press has no responsibility for the persistence or
accuracy of URLs for external or third-party internet websites referred to in
this publication, and does not guarantee that any content on such websites is,
or will remain, accurate or appropriate.

PREFATORY NOTE

THE two earlier of these discourses were preached on 13th January and 21st July 1918, and formed part of a series of sermons by laymen given in St Edward's Church, Cambridge. The last was preached in King's College Chapel on 26th January 1919, after the return to the University of many undergraduates who had been serving in the war.

They are published together as they are concerned with one aspect—the religious aspect—of a problem which is in all men's minds at the present time.

CONTENTS

I

LIFE

For as we have many members in one body,
and all members have not the same office:
so we, being many, are one body in Christ,
and every one members one of another.

Rom. xii. 4, 5.

"WE, being many, are one body." The Apostle
was writing to men whom he had never seen—to
the members of the small Christian community at
Rome—and he said that he and they together
formed one body. This comparison of a society of
men to the living body of an animal, with its
various parts and organs, was not new even when
he wrote, and it is so common now that we are
apt to miss its meaning. There are controversies
as to how far the analogy carries us when it is
applied to any community—to the family, the
township, the State, or the Church. With these
controversies most of us do not concern ourselves.
But we are familiar with the phrase "the body
politic" to describe the State, and we let it pass

without thinking; and we have even come to use the word "body" as simply a noun of multitude, signifying many, for any collection or aggregate, so that we are accustomed to speak of a "body of men" when we are referring only to some haphazard gathering of human beings.

We are thus in danger of overlooking the meaning of the phrase through familiarity with the words. But, when St Paul said "We, being many, are one body," he meant exactly what he said, neither more nor less. How fraught with significance his utterance was may be seen from the words which go before it and from those which follow it. It is the centre of his whole doctrine of the Christian Church and of the Christian life. How deeply the thought had struck its roots into his mind is shown from its occurrence in his letters not to Rome only but to the Christian communities elsewhere—at Corinth, at Ephesus, and at Colosse. Let us attempt then to recover some fragments of his meaning and see whether it applies to our own time as well as to his.

The analogy had been used before to describe the nature of a political society or State; but he was the first to use it of the Christian society or

Church, and in doing so he gave it a new depth of meaning. He has made it distinctively Pauline. It does not appear to have been used by the other New Testament writers. It is also absent from the reported sayings of our Lord. Perhaps his parables show a preference for illustrating the kingdom of heaven by analogies drawn from life rather than from inanimate things. But all the familiar experiences of daily routine are put under contribution by him: most of all the human relationships of family and business and neighbourhood; also the life of the fields and of the sea—the mustard-seed, the vine and figtree and the fishes; and again the lifeless things that minister to men's wants—the garment, the piece of silver, the pearl of great price.

As long as the Master was with them, the disciples did not need any elaborate explanation of the new community which was being formed. He was there, their leader and guide, to direct each step and answer every question as it arose. When his bodily presence was withdrawn how was the void to be filled? It was of the very essence of his mission that he could have no successor as an earthly monarch has, or as other religious teachers

1—2

such as Mahomet have left behind them. When the shepherd was gone how were the flock to be led? One result seems to have been that the members of the orphaned church were drawn more closely together. They shared their worldly goods with one another, had all things in common, and waited for the second coming of the Lord from heaven. Thus the disciples were made to feel that they were indeed members one of another, and were prepared to receive the words of St Paul that they, being many, were yet one body.

St Paul does not discard other illustrations of the truth which he has in view. In particular he often uses the old analogy of a building. "Ye are God's building[1]," he tells the Corinthians; and to the Ephesians he says that they "are built upon the foundation of the apostles and prophets, Jesus Christ himself being the chief corner stone; in whom all the building fitly framed together groweth unto an holy temple in the Lord[2]." This was the old and approved comparison sanctioned by the Old Testament writers: "Behold, I lay in Zion for a foundation a stone, a tried stone, a precious corner stone, a

[1] 1 Cor. iii. 9.   [2] Eph. ii. 20.

sure foundation[1]." The comparison suited a people
for whom Jerusalem was the city of promise and
whose worship centred in the Temple. It was
used by our Lord in the parable of the house
built upon a rock; and we find it again in the
"city which hath foundations[2]" of the Epistle to
the Hebrews, and in the imaginative description
of the New Jerusalem, the holy city descending
out of heaven from God, given in the Revelation
of St John. But our Lord's death made a break
with Judaism; the Temple could no longer be the
shrine of the disciples' worship; even Jerusalem
ceased to be the home to which they must look
to return. These things remained a memory and
they became an ideal: Christians were to fashion
themselves into a spiritual temple; a new Jerusalem was to come down from heaven. And so it
is that St Paul's language overruns the old analogy:
he speaks of the Church *growing* into a holy temple
in the Lord. Now an analogy must never be
pressed beyond the point which it illustrates.
When the Church is spoken of as a building, the
emphasis is usually on its stability, and hence the
stress laid on the foundation, the corner stone,

[1] Isaiah xxviii. 16. [2] Heb. xi. 10.

in so many passages. The building is also a unity of many parts and may be taken as the symbol of the household or community which it shelters. But the analogy conveys nothing as to the life of the community; and so, when we speak of its growth, our thought is really seeking out another and deeper analogy—the analogy with the living body.

Life can be likened only to life. If we are looking for an image whereto to compare the life of a community whether civil or religious we can only find it in some other thing which is also living—in the plant, or the animal, or the man. The building can at most bring before us the shell, the skeleton, or the material vesture of that which lives. Even a machine, however cunningly devised, cannot do more than indicate how parts are put together and what sort of work they can turn out. You can take a machine to pieces and put it together again; but you cannot do that with the living organism. If one part is worn or broken you can replace it by another like part made at a factory; but it is not so with the animal body. There the hurt of one member is the hurt of the whole: it cannot be scrapped and replaced by a

new member of the same kind. The life comes
from within and lives in every member, so that
the hurt of one is the hurt of all and the health
of the whole body is the health of each part. As
St Paul said in his earlier and fuller discourse on
this topic in the first Epistle to the Corinthians,
"whether one member suffer all the members
suffer with it; or one member be honoured all the
members rejoice with it[1]." And the same holds of
the life of the community. If one member suffer
all the members suffer with it; in the honour of
one member all the members share. The more
truly a number of men form a community, and
not a mere chance collection of individuals or
battle-ground of selfish interests, the more fully
is the doctrine verified. We realise it better now
in these critical days of war, than we did before
in the piping times of peace, when men thought
that as things had been so they would continue to
be and when each strove to lay up goods for
himself for many years. Now we know that we
stand or fall together: the suffering of one part
is felt by all; the success of any is the triumph
of all.

[1] 1 Cor. xii. 26.

There is but one task for all—
For each one life to give.
Who stands if freedom fall?
Who dies if England live?

And the crisis often forces us to put to ourselves the question, Who lives if England die? Most perhaps would be inclined to answer that in such a case life would have nothing of value to offer. With this country crushed and a calculated ruthlessness supreme in the world, we should not care to go on living, because something had been killed in the soul of England, and in our own souls—the best thing which is its and ours—the heritage of freedom and the hope of a nobler future for the spirit of man. These are spiritual things; and if the spirit is dead, in man or in society, the life has gone out.

Here we touch the central point of St Paul's teaching. It is the common life which makes the body a unity of many members. Each member has its own work to do; but they all serve one body and are sustained by a single life. "The eye cannot say unto the hand, I have no need of thee; nor again the head to the feet, I have no need of you[1]"; but each should have the same care one

[1] 1 Cor. xii. 21.

of another so that there "be no schism in the
body[1]." It is the same in the Church: there are
"diversities of gifts," "differences of administra-
tions," "diversities of operations[2]." And to each
his own duty: "whether prophecy, let us prophesy
according to the proportion of faith; or ministry,
let us wait on our ministering: or he that teacheth,
on teaching; or he that exhorteth, on exhortation:
he that giveth, let him do it with simplicity;
he that ruleth, with diligence; he that sheweth
mercy, with cheerfulness[3]." The work is manifold,
as the members are many; but they all spring out
of one spiritual life. For "all these worketh that
one and the self-same Spirit, dividing to every
man severally as he will[4]." In this spirit is the
common life and energy that animate the whole
community, so that through it diversities of gifts
and operations conspire to the common good:
"we, being many, are one body in Christ."

The spirit which was to achieve the unity and
prove the power of the Christian community was
simply the spirit of Christ. Whatever the differences between the members of the Church, that

---

[1] 1 Cor. xii. 25.   [2] 1 Cor. xii. 4–6.
[3] Rom. xii. 6–8.   [4] 1 Cor. xii. 11.

spirit held them together by a common memory and sustained them by a common hope. The memory was the earthly life and death and resurrection of Jesus; the hope was the expectation of his second coming in the clouds from heaven. What must have been their feelings as year after year disappointed this hope and the Lord still delayed his coming? This we cannot tell. But we know that the hope in its old form, as the early disciples held it, has faded and died away with the lapse of centuries. We know also that, as it disappeared in this form, the deeper elements of St Paul's teaching made their way into men's minds, and they became aware of a spiritual force that might regenerate the world and establish on earth the kingdom of heaven.

This spiritual hope has never died out in the Church, and it has never entirely deserted mankind. Sometimes it has lain dormant, usually in periods of external comfort, when the easy ways of the world obscured it; and it has needed the shock of danger or of disaster to awaken it anew. In the world's day-light it has been a pillar of cloud which men could easily disregard, but in the gloom of some great calamity it has often shone

like a pillar of fire. And now, in the midnight of
their misery, men of all nations turn their eyes
towards the brighter hope. In our own country
the air is full of the expectation of the new world
which is to succeed the present turmoil, and of
preparation for it. Every one is called upon to
take his share in this preparation; and the word
Reconstruction is on all men's lips. Yet the very
word gives us pause and suggests reflexions. It is
the Old Testament metaphor of the building that
is used, not the New Testament metaphor of the
living body. And what is needed at the present
juncture is not so much the re-building of an
edifice as the renewal of life. Has it ever occurred
to us that, in all his discourses concerning the
coming of the kingdom, our Lord never said,
Society must be reconstructed, or The world must
be rebuilt? What he said was, Man must be born
again—born of the spirit. Unless the spirit is renewed what does the fashion of the building matter?
They begin at the wrong end who plan first the
shape and size of the house without giving thought
to the life that is to dwell therein. "Except the Lord
build the house they labour in vain that build it[1]."

[1] Psalm cxxvii. 1.

We need not depreciate the importance of the "problems of reconstruction," as they are called. But the first problem is the problem of the Spirit. In what spirit are we to live our lives in the days that are coming? All the other problems follow upon this. If we could solve it, their solution also would be easy. If we really sought and obtained the kingdom of God and his righteousness, all other things would be added to us. They are the accessories; it is the essence—the spirit of the new life. St Paul's earliest comparison of the Christian community to a living body is followed immediately by his great hymn in praise of love. Love is the spirit of Christ. If it really animated the body of his church or the body of the people, our social difficulties would be insignificant. Without it we do not overcome these difficulties; we only invent palliatives for them; and sometimes our artifices may hinder the working of the spirit of love which they should encourage.

When Reconstruction is our cry we form plans which are large and simple, and in forming them we are often under the power of catchwords. A short time ago equality of opportunity was demanded; then, when the toll of war had to be paid, it was equality of sacrifice. There is often reason behind these catchwords. It is true that there are many inequalities at present which are unnecessary and hurtful and which a wiser administration would remove. For the most part they are the legacy of a time of great mechanical inventions, when energetic men joined in the race for wealth, using their simpler fellow-mortals as tools to minister to their greed, and when the State supinely held aloof. These inequalities are a disease of the body politic, and a healthy constitution will throw them off. But the call for complete equality, whether of opportunity or of sacrifice, is a call to substitute mechanism for life. All the bricks in a house may be of the same pattern and have much the same use. But society is not like a house. It is more like the living organism in which unlikeness in the members is needed for the unity and health of the body. This is the case with the nation also. One member does what other members cannot do; but all may serve, all may help the common life. The ideal of equality is legitimate if it be taken as a protest against those who evade their duties or try to make a profit out of the necessities of their country.

But it is unhealthy and disastrous if it lead men—
as it sometimes does—to look to what others are
doing, instead of trying to do all they can themselves, and to count the efforts and the losses of
others lest haply their own should be greater. We
cannot really measure these things; and when we
attempt to do them by measure we kill the spirit
both of enterprise and of sacrifice. No life worthy
of the name can be lived by the ledger of profit
and loss:

> High heaven rejects the lore
> Of nicely-calculated less or more.

We are all sharers in a larger life than our own;
and the more fully we share it—the greater our
"measure of faith," as the Apostle puts it—the
less shall we be inclined to count our own efforts
or even our own sufferings as an expenditure
which must not exceed the similar efforts or
sacrifices of others. We have only to look around
and abroad to see that equality is not and could
not be a feature of our universe. The call comes
to men in different ways and for different work.
It is not possible, for instance, to compare our
own small discomforts with the sufferings of the
soldier in the firing line, who spends his days in

hourly peril of death till the supreme moment
comes and his sacrifice is completed. He does not
give by measure: he gives himself to that greater
life which includes him and us: if our freedom is
secured it will be through his sacrifice; and his
example should show us how to use that freedom.
He is still a member of that spiritual body which
we are: death cannot sever him from it. And, when
the enterprise is over, he will be with us in spirit;

> When Te Deums seek the skies,
> When the Organ shakes the Dome,
> A dead man shall stand
> At each live man's hand—
> For they also have come home.

The experiences of the last three years have
brought home to us, as we never felt it before, the
kinship of the living and the dead. Those who
have gone before have both part and lot in our
inheritance. They will have nothing to say about
"plans of reconstruction"; but we shall do them
wrong unless we build in their spirit: and their's
was not the calculating spirit. It heard the call
of the greater life to which it belonged, and it
obeyed the call not counting the cost.

Last Sunday, in this church and in every church

throughout the land, a solemn service of inter-
cession was held in behalf of the nation and empire
in this time of war. Our prayer was that God
would hasten the coming of his kingdom—the
kingdom which is righteousness and peace among
men. This kingdom must begin in our hearts and
be established through our wills. Where are the
signs of its coming? Have the tribulations of these
last years worked in us the peaceable fruits of
righteousness—the righteousness among whose
fruits is peace among men? We, whom age or
infirmity of whatever kind has debarred from
service abroad, have been spared the physical
sufferings endured steadfastly by the men at the
front. It is humiliating to think that grumblings
should be heard from any of us at the petty
material troubles we may be called upon to bear.
It is for us to support our advanced guard not only
by material supplies but in spirit; and it is also
our task to see to it that their home-coming shall
be to a country made worthy of the safety which
they have bought at so terrible a price. The men
who marched away left a great trust in our keeping.
Let it not be said that, when the war of nations
is over, they are to return to a war of classes pre-

pared for them by the men who stayed at home. It is our part to fight and overcome the forces of selfishness and luxury among ourselves which make for division, and to foster the spirit of love, which "seeketh not her own," from which both the body politic and the body ecclesiastical draw their life. In this spirit we shall conquer, and through it the country may be made a fit dwelling-place for a renewed life. But in this spiritual conflict, as in material warfare, victory comes only to those who are ready and strong to fight and who are determined to fight to a finish. The sword of the spirit must never be sheathed till the spiritual cause is won.

> I will not cease from mental fight,
>   Nor shall my sword sleep in my hand,
> Till we have built Jerusalem
>   In England's green and pleasant land.

II

FAITH

> If ye have faith as a grain of mustard seed,
> ye shall say unto this mountain, Remove
> hence to yonder place; and it shall remove;
> and nothing shall be impossible unto you.
> Matt. xvii. 20.

THE words are arresting, provocative even. They may easily seem to make too great a demand upon our faith. But they do not stand alone. The power of faith is often emphasised in the New Testament in terms that seem to set no bounds to it. Over and over again our Lord himself appeals to some answering faith in a man's soul, to which even nature yields, and without which his own work is of no avail. It was her faith that made whole the woman with the issue of blood[1]; it was because of the greatness of her faith that the prayer of the Canaanitish woman was heard and her daughter restored to her[2]; it was her faith and not the alabaster box that saved the woman

[1] Matt. ix. 22.   [2] Matt. xv. 28.

which was a sinner[1]; when the two blind men had their sight restored to them, it was with the words, "According to your faith be it unto you[2]." And on the other hand, when faith failed in his hearers, Christ's power was stayed: in his own country, where the prophet was without honour, "he did not many mighty works there because of their unbelief[3]."

What Christ said of particular occasions his disciples repeated and generalised. Witness the record in the Epistle to the Hebrews of those "who through faith subdued kingdoms, wrought righteousness, obtained promises, stopped the mouths of lions, quenched the violence of fire, escaped the edge of the sword, out of weakness were made strong, waxed valiant in fight, turned to flight the armies of the aliens[4]." But this triumphant record is not more impressive than the simple words of the text—that for faith nothing is impossible, that it can remove mountains.

Is all this to be put down to Oriental exaggeration? It may be that the phrase in the text is imaginative, but its meaning is not merely

[1] Luke vii. 50.   [2] Matt. ix. 29.
[3] Matt. xiii. 58.   [4] Heb. xi. 33, 34.

Eastern. "East is east and west is west"; yet the twain do meet. There is the same world of law and order surrounding them, and human nature is one. The statement is a paradox, if you will— something that goes flat against ordinary opinion; but it is in such paradoxes that the deepest truth is often expressed. The meaning is clear: that faith gives a power of meeting danger and over- coming difficulty, and that there are no limits which we can assign to this power. The words in which the meaning is expressed arrest the atten- tion, and have formed the subject of many dis- courses. But this is not the point on which I wish to speak to-day. The paradox of the power of faith has occupied us so much that we are apt to overlook another and greater paradox in this verse—the paradox of the nature of faith. What is that faith that can remove mountains? we ask. And the answer is that it is faith "as a grain of mustard seed." This, too, is a hard saying; how are we to understand it?

The great procession of the faithful, which moves through the Epistle to the Hebrews, is composed of the leaders of Israel and of the earlier heroes who connected Israel with the beginnings

of our race. We see there Abel and Enoch and
Noah, Abraham and the patriarchs, Moses and
the judges, David also and Samuel and the
prophets. They seem to march with waving
banners and to the sound of trumpets. They are
the great men of the world, the mighty of the
Lord, called up to witness to the power of faith,
though the promise was yet to come. But when
our Lord speaks of faith, he chooses humbler
examples. Not many mighty, not many noble,
are cited by him. He does not select the learned
class; what he meant by faith he found lacking in
scribes and pharisees, strict as was their orthodoxy.
He even went beyond the circle of Judaism, to
the Roman centurion and the Canaanitish woman;
beyond the pale of health and righteousness, to
the weak and to the erring, to the woman with
the issue of blood and to Mary Magdalene. He
did not limit it to the grown-up and mature in
mind: he "called a little child unto him, and set
him in the midst of them[1]."

If we saw these pass before us in procession,
how different would it be from that other procession of the Epistle to the Hebrews! The alien

[1] Matt. xviii. 2.

and the ignorant, the blind and the lame, the paralytic and the leper, the diseased and the harlot, and a little child in their midst. No trumpets herald their approach, no banners wave along their line. Unknown to the world, unnoticed in the crowd—men without name and women without reputation—they pass with feeble steps before unobservant eyes. Yet, could we read the heart, a secret would be revealed in them all which makes them more powerful than the mighty, wiser than the learned, better than the righteous. What is this mystery of faith that so subverts all our accustomed values?

It is not produced by social tradition—the powerful selection of history that forces a community to struggle for its life or to disappear. This is not the source of faith—often, indeed, it is its grave. Christ found faith dead in the Jewish Church, loyal as its members were to their traditions. In later times those nearest his spirit have often had cause to lament its decay within the Church he founded. It may be sought in vain in learning and the culture of the intellect. In spite of all that these have done to glorify the mind of man, the new wisdom of the Greek is no more the

source and guardian of faith than the outworn
tradition of the Jew. To one it may be a
stumbling-block, to the other foolishness. It is
not even the offspring of the normal maturity of
human powers, as these are ripened by experience
of self and of the world. The wise and prudent
may miss it; it may be revealed to babes. Deep
in the heart of man, deeper than the heart of man,
Christ finds its roots. So deep, that he goes below
human nature itself for an instance of it—down to
the very germ and principle of natural life. The
faith to which nothing is impossible, the faith that
can remove mountains, is likened to the faith
possessed by a grain of mustard seed.

Herein lies the paradox. There is something on
which the health of man's soul and his power over
the world depend; and we ask, Where is it to be
found? Let us see it at its purest and strongest.
For answer we are given an example; but that
example is not taken from the mind of any upon
whom we are wont to look as prominent or powerful—the statesman, or warrior, or philosopher,
the king or the priest. It is not even taken from
the mind of the plain man, who is sometimes
encouraged to believe that ignorance is a guide to

perfection. We are pointed to the least of the seeds of the field. What is the meaning of this paradox? How can the faith of a man be likened to anything that goes on in the mustard seed?

For an explanation we are forced back upon something very simple, very primitive. The seed which is cast into the ground has a unique faculty belonging to it: it can live and grow. But it is not sufficient for itself. Separate it from its surroundings in nature, and it will only shrivel and die. It must draw its strength from the soil in which it is planted: it is rooted in mother earth, watered by the rains of heaven, warmed by the sun. The secret of its life is its own; but its strength comes from the greater world to which it belongs. For it all things are possible—all things, that is, that belong to its nature. It is "the least of all seeds: but when it is grown, it is the greatest among herbs, and becometh a tree, so that the birds of the air come and lodge in the branches thereof[1]." In this way it perfects itself and plays its allotted part in the world. But at each stage of its growth, and to preserve its vegetable life, it draws upon the sustenance pro-

[1] Matt. xiii. 32.

vided by its environment. So it fulfils its nature,
and beyond its nature it neither grows nor seeks
to grow. And thus we may picture its life from
seed to tree—a life of constant reliance on the
sustenance of mother earth, unbroken by discord
or doubt, growing from strength to strength in
harmony and peace.

It is this reliance on something greater than
oneself—something which supports and animates
one's own life and gives it strength to achieve and
to endure—that is the bottom-character of faith.
True, the faith of a man is not as the faith of a
seed or a tree. Man, it may be, if you look solely
on his outward frame, is but a reed shaken by the
winds; but yet, as Pascal said, he is a thinking
reed and therefore greater than the winds that
buffet him. In the whole of nature he stands
apart, in it and yet not altogether of it: not a
mere child of nature, but thinking his own thoughts
and choosing his own way. He may not simply
imitate, he cannot easily attain, the effortless
harmony which he sees around him in nature. As
he looks round on universal nature he sees it lapped
in universal law: the hill bends to the valley, and
the tree sways in the wind; life and death them-

selves go hand in hand; and each natural object follows its appointed path, as the stars fulfil their courses, "still quiring to the young-eyed cherubims."

> Peace sleeps the earth upon,
> And sweet peace on the hill.
> The waves that whimper still
> At their long law-serving
> (O flowing sad complaint!)
> Come on and are back drawn.
> Man only owns no king,
> Man only is not faint.

For earth is not his master, nor the sole nourisher of his life; he has other laws to fulfil than those of nature.

Herein lies the explanation of the paradox. The things of nature move as their own nature dictates and in unquestioned dependence on their surroundings. There is nothing in them which disturbs their reliance on the world and its laws. They do not strive or cry. Their faith, if we may call it so, is untouched by doubt. On its own level it is more absolute than any faith to which man attains. But then it is on a far lower level than his. It is man's privilege to look out on the world and judge it as if it were something to which he himself did not belong. The order of nature gives no sure support for the life of mind. He must strive to attain that reliance, that harmony, which is the birthright of every living thing that belongs to nature only; his effort and frequent failures are uttered in his cry. A man's faith, therefore, must be suited to his character as a free and rational being. But it is not, on that account, something specially intellectual. We must not confuse *faith in* some one with *belief that* a certain doctrine is true. The latter is an affair of the intellect alone. The former is the attitude of the whole man, when he trusts another—often without being able to express in words the grounds for that trust.

We are told to add to our faith virtue, and to virtue knowledge[1]. Faith is the principle of life; virtue and knowledge should follow upon it; and the kind of faith a man lives by is shown in his character and in his way of thinking. Thus it has come about that those, whose special duty it is to be guardians of the faith, have always sought at the same time to promote virtuous conduct and to promulgate sound doctrine. The latter has been the business of the theologians. They have worked

---

[1] 2 Pet. i. 5.

out a system of doctrines which have been, and must needs be, set forth in terms that appeal to the intellect. Thus the creeds have been formed and accepted and repeated.

The process may have been necessary and in some cases illuminating; but it has reacted upon the faith from which it sprang, and these reactions have not always been salutary. We are apt to forget the difference between the living faith, which may find utterance in a doctrine, and the mere acceptance of that doctrine because handed down by authority. We even tend sometimes to forget the difference between believing the doctrine and repeating the words in which it is expressed. And so creeds and catechisms come to be learned by rote and repeated with energy, but not always with understanding. At this stage, the process may show submission of the intellect; it is certainly not knowledge; it is very far from being faith—such as we have found faith to be; and it would be hard to show that it is of any value at all. There is no virtue in a form of words. You cannot remove mountains by repeating a formula: that is the way of magic, not the way of religion. Yet, are we sure that it is not sometimes our way?

Even if we understand the meaning and our intellect gives assent to the creed, that is not the same thing as a living faith. We say or recite "I believe in God the Father"; but do we realise all that we are saying? Is it a real experience or only an intellectual assertion? Do we rest our minds and wills on his and draw on his love for our strength? Or are we simply making the bald metaphysical statement that in our opinion heaven and earth had an almighty architect? "And in Jesus Christ his only son our Lord." Do we realise that in him human nature touched the divine and that we are brought into union with God through him? and have we ourselves trodden any part of the way which he opened? Or are we only making a number of statements which we have learned, in which fact and symbol are curiously entangled? "He descended into hell." Have we ourselves, in the darkest hour of our calamity, found him beside us in the depths, our comfort and support? Or are we merely giving voice to strange speculations about the after-life? "He ascended into heaven." Do our souls rise to his? "I believe in the Holy Ghost." Have we felt the spirit animating our souls, renewing our life, giving us strength to do and suffer all things? If so, we have had some experience of faith; if not, might we not as well go on discussing the *filioque* clause? "The Communion of Saints." Is it a reality for us or a name? "The forgiveness of sins." Have we experienced it or the need of it? "And the life everlasting." Does it really affect our present conduct, or do we carry on·on the maxim that one world is enough at a time?

We might almost say that the creed has two different meanings—a meaning for life and a meaning for the intellect. Only, this would be to draw too absolute a distinction; for intellect is one expression of life, and the life of the spirit is never without understanding. But the intellect tends to go its own way and to refine upon its notions until they lose all touch with life as we experience it. These refinements may have some significance for the rare theological reasoners in whom thinking seems to have usurped the place of living; but they lose all meaning in the hands of the followers who repeat or confute the shibboleths of their predecessors. Thus theology outruns religion, and dogma takes the place of faith.

It is easy to emphasise overmuch the intellectual side of faith, and the Church has suffered from the tendency. Christian doctrine is made into a system which cannot be entered by those untrained in intellectual subtleties, however deep their Christian experience; and, as an offset to this, people are encouraged to think that learning a formula is a necessary requisite for religion, if not a sufficient substitute for it. And again, the process is apt to overlook the variety of the Christian life, and to fix into the form of dogma characteristics which are drawn from the peculiarities of some particular historical movement or some particular class of minds. The doctrines, which in this way register one phase of experience only, come to be promulgated as essential to the faith, and ecclesiastical authority is invoked to confine the workings of the spirit within the four corners of an intellectual scheme. This is one cause—perhaps the chief cause—of there being divisions among us; and the conflict of the creeds destroys the unity of the faith.

All this comes of laying too great stress on the intellectual side of faith—on the doctrines which have been drawn from it by the theologians. It is true that faith has and must have an intellectual side—like everything else that concerns man. The faith of a man cannot, like that of the mustard seed, consist in unthinking dependence on something else. As it is said, "he that cometh to God must believe that he is[1]." But surely we are not justified in saying that he must also believe some particular system of doctrines which theologians have distilled into the creeds—for controversy among the learned and to the confusion of the simple. Would not the apostles themselves have been puzzled if they had been asked to consent *ex animo* to the Thirty-nine Articles? The Master took his examples of faith from humble folk; and the Church should follow his lead, lest perchance it shut out from its fold any of those who are children of God by faith[2]. He never demanded that his hearers should assent to theological doctrines disconnected with their own experience. He asked faith of them; he needed their faith to heal and save them. But it was simply faith in God as the father and giver of life and faith in himself as the love and power of God made manifest. This is the essence of our faith, that we

---

[1] Heb. xi. 6. [2] Gal. iii. 26.

should trust in the spirit of God which enables us to do and bear all things. And this is the essence of Christian doctrine, that we should know Christ as revealing the Father and reconciling man with God. If, going beyond these simple truths, we seek to impose intellectual burdens upon others, we should bear in mind that there are more ways than one of making the word of God of none effect through our traditions.

III

VISION

And I saw a new heaven and a new earth:
for the first heaven and the first earth were
passed away. Rev. xxi. 1.

THE New Testament as it has been handed down
to us closes with a vision of the last things. Visions
of this sort were common in the writings of the
later centuries of the old era and in the beginning
of our own. Within the Canon they stretch back
to the Book of Daniel and they reach a climax in
the Revelation of St John; and they are recognised
as forming a special type of literature. But this
type was only a concentrated expression of a
factor which belonged to the prophetic spirit and
appealed to the popular mind. It was characteristic of the Hebrews as a race that they looked
forwards not backwards. Their golden age was not
in the past but in the future. They believed that
God had made a Covenant with them and that he
was preparing them for its fulfilment. They were

always on the march to a promised land, from the
day that Abraham went out not knowing whither
he went. His faith was great but his vision was
feeble. Afterwards the vision grew in definiteness,
sometimes losing touch with the faith that inspired
it. At first the country which the people sought
was a place of material comforts, a land flowing
with milk and honey. Time and experience altered
the outlook. Their Zion was to be an inheritance
of the righteous, a city of God, and God himself
was to lead them there. When the nation was
crushed by a series of disasters, they still looked
for a Redeemer who was to restore and extend their
prosperity. But when the Messiah came, as the
kingdom comes, without observation, and himself
suffered and died, they were no longer able to
trust in the slow evolution of their national destiny:
they looked for something catastrophic—a violent
overthrow of all earthly powers and a speedy
coming of the Son of Man in the clouds from
heaven. All the resources of an Oriental imagination were utilised to depict the struggle of the
higher and the lower powers for the mastery of
man, until the final defeat of the powers of evil:
and then Jerusalem was not to be re-built on

earth but should come down new from heaven, and the everlasting reign of righteousness would begin. For this consummation they awaited in eager expectation: and, in spite of the long periods of time through which the struggle was pictured as lasting, the book ends with the prayer and the promise that the Lord would come quickly.

In this and similar visions we must keep our eyes on the essentials. But it is the accidental details that strike us first; and generations of commentators have flattered curious minds with vain predictions. Our imagination is attracted by the scenery of the picture: it follows the incidents of the combat, and dwells on the dazzling structure of the city that is to descend from heaven. Yet all these things are merely externals. The ground of contention and of hope lies far deeper. It is not the scarlet robe but the abomination it covers that gives its wearer her temporary power and leads to her final overthrow. And the white horse is but an emblem of the purity of him who was called Faithful and True and who judged and made war in righteousness. Throughout the whole vision we are confronted by the old alternative of Mount Gerizim and Mount Ebal—on the one hand life

and good, on the other death and evil[1]. The seer
has the world-old conflict before his eyes, he sees
it come to an issue, and he has confidence in the
final triumph of the good. It is the same with his
view of what is to happen after the battle is won.
The jewelled walls and golden pavements of the
New Jerusalem may leave us cold: they are the
toys of an earlier, more child-like mind. But we
need the reminder that after war comes peace,
that the victory over evil means a reign of
righteousness, that for him that overcometh glory
is reserved.

It is possible certainly to dissociate the two
things—the insight into spiritual forces and the
vision, or pretended vision, of future events. And
they have often been divorced. A superstitious
populace is less easily impressed by insight into
life than by a picture of things to come. It was
the latter that first attracted them to the prophet;
they treated him as a seer and called him by that
name[2]. It was always hard to make them listen
to the message with the same zeal as they would
consult the vision. And men were to be found in
the schools of the prophets who would give them

---

[1] Deut. xxx. 15.   [2] 1 Sam. ix. 9.

what they asked for—chaff instead of wheat—
and minister to curiosity without feeding the soul.
"Yea, they are prophets of the deceit of their
own heart; which think to cause my people to
forget my name by their dreams[1]." Perhaps the
greatest enemy of true religion has, all along, been
the claim to vision which is not based on an
understanding of the really vital forces of history.
Especially in periods of crisis and calamity,
troubled minds have always been eager to see
behind the veil; and, from the time of the witch
of Endor to the London medium of our own day,
they have found instruments willing to pierce it
for them—at a price. The test of all these revela-
tions is their result. They picture the world
beyond as a pale reflexion of the material condi-
tions of the present. And they show no genuine
vision, for they have no real insight into the
moral forces which now fight for mastery and in
which lies the promise of the future.

There is all the difference between the two
kinds of vision. One is the prophetic vision, which
comes from insight into the spiritual forces which
rule the world. It gives visible form to spiritual

---

[1] Jer. xxiii. 26, 27.

ideas because it has been able to discover the significance of actual events. The other deals with more superficial aspects. It draws from external features and projects a fancy picture into the future. The one gives promise of a higher life; the other has no meaning beyond the material things which it represents.

In the perplexities of the present time our way will be guided by the vision of things hoped for; and it will be well with us only if the vision is of the former kind—if it is based upon insight into the forces of righteousness. Again and again, during these four and a half years we were encouraged by the belief that we were fighting on the side of right and that the right would in the end prevail. We were animated by this belief when we first took up the gage of battle; we were sustained by it through long days of disappointed hope; and now our faith has been justified by the issue.

Still greater enterprise lies before us. The problems of peace are more difficult than those of war. The trumpet which summoned to battle gave no uncertain sound, and the nation answered it as one man: other interests were overwhelmed by the insistent question of life or death for the country. We have now to restore the life that has been saved, to re-build a world better than the old; and our advisers have many voices but fail to give one clear call. We are even in danger of forgetting the faith by which we conquered. That faith was two-fold: that the things of greatest worth in life are not material things but moral and spiritual, and that these moral and spiritual values are also in the long run the strongest forces. The imponderables gather weight and gain the mastery over the merely material and ponderable. So it has happened; so it will happen again. As we face the shadowy future our faith in this must be pure and our courage firm to risk putting our faith to the test. In the effort after reconstruction, whether in State, in Church, or in College, we should follow the spiritual vision.

But let us not deceive ourselves. There is another vision than this—a vision that obscures these higher values—and there are many who follow it. It is no easy peace that lies before us, but a new conflict—a greater conflict than that from which we are emerging, a conflict of ideals. Are the spiritual values truly the greatest things in life or are they fanciful and unreal, as compared with the solid facts of material comfort? In their thoroughgoing way the Continental Socialists have faced this question, and the great majority of them have adopted a frankly materialistic view of what is worth having in life. Their creed has been elevated into a philosophy, and it is supported by many scholars who see in human life only a struggle for material gain, who put forward an economic interpretation of history, and who base their vision for the future on this reading of the past. The same tendency is not so hardened or so widespread in our own country, but it is not negligible, and with us also the secular interpretation of life threatens to displace the religious.

This tendency is not a characteristic of one class of society only; it belongs to all classes, and to almost everyone in some portions of his activity. There is indeed a counsel of perfection, "Seek ye first the kingdom of God and his righteousness; and all these things shall be added unto you[1]." But it is not often followed, even by those who applaud it. We are more inclined to make sure of the other things, before troubling about the king-

[1] Matt. vi. 33.

dom and its righteousness. It would seem to be the law—or paradox, if you will—of human life that the higher values can make their appeal to men only after some measure of the lower values has been reached. And then the struggle for these lower but necessary values becomes so keen that men can think of nothing else. It is of the very nature of material things to engender strife. The lower the good, the more contentious it is. Material goods are exclusive in their possession and in their enjoyment. What one man has, another wants and tries to get. It is not so with the goods of the mind. Truth and beauty and goodness can be shared by all. Their possession by one man helps instead of hindering their attainment by others. They are not like material goods subject to the law of diminishing returns; they follow a law of their own—a law of increasing returns. The more men's affections are set on these higher goods, the truer will be their appreciation of the lower goods of life which form their necessary substratum; the readier also will they be to carry out a distribution of them which is juster and more generous than that which has resulted from our selfish competitive system. Thus, in the end, our industrial salvation will depend on the character of the men whom the new order produces and on the estimate they form of what things are of greatest worth in life.

The Church has from of old been the guardian of the higher spiritual values—on which the measurement of all other values depends. It does not any longer control learning and science, education and industry in the way it once did. Yet it cannot hold aloof from these interests, lest religion be divorced from life. In particular it is concerned with the things of the mind, and it has courageously raised the question of its own relation to the intellectual life of the people. When the late Dr Benson was appointed to the see of Canterbury, his friend Dr Hort wrote him a remarkable letter. It was not exactly a letter of congratulation. He called it a letter of sympathy. It was also a note of warning—a warning of rocks ahead. "The danger for the English Church," he wrote, "is its calm and unobtrusive alienation in thought and spirit from the great silent multitude of Englishmen[1]." Thirty-six years have passed since these words were written, and in the last

[1] F. J. A. Hort's *Life and Letters*, ii. 290.

years of this period the Church has had a great opportunity. The most devoted and clear-sighted of its younger clergy have accompanied the great silent multitude to the field of battle. They have stood beside them and ministered to them in the elemental crises of danger and violent death, when the conventional hypocrisies fall away from a man like a garment. They have seen their souls naked. And they have come home and told us how far the alienation in thought and spirit has gone.

The Archbishops too have not been idle. They have appointed a number of committees to enquire into the whole life and work of the Church; and these committees have issued a series of most instructive reports. One of the committees has dealt with this particular subject. It confirms the opinion of the chaplains and investigates the causes of the alienation. "While there has been an increase in the intellectual attainments of the people," they say, "the intellectual capacity and equipment of the clergy have not increased in a like proportion." "There has been a tendency to contrast the intellectual with the spiritual, instead of realising that God's spirit works in man by illuminating all his powers, and that the highest spiritual work is also intellectual. The result has been a depreciation and a fear of the honest operation of the intellect." Hence "intellectual sloth and indecision" and "lack of intellectual courage," while "the interest of the clergy is often drawn away to questions of secondary importance. They are engrossed in minor matters of Church tradition, and do not speak in a real and living manner on great and fundamental problems which are exercising the minds of many people at the present day[1]." "Science has much learning behind it; the weight of learning in the Church of England is inadequate, and therefore the Church's authority is weakened[2]." "The interest of the Church has been turned from the intellectual problems[3]"; "fewer able men seek ordination[4]"; and their position in the universities is weakened.

What is the reason of this divorce between intellect and the Church? The Committee give several reasons, but they scarcely venture to touch upon one which is surely not the least important. They refer to "the uncertainty that young men feel about the truth of Christianity and matters

---

[1] *Report of the Archbishops' First Committee*, p. 8.
[2] *Ibid.* p. 10.   [3] *Ibid.* p. 8.   *Ibid.* p. 9.

of theology"—"a feeling of uncertainty which often checks very suitable men whose spiritual aims dispose them to seek ordination[1]." But they fail to draw a necessary distinction—a distinction which may be expressed in their own words as that between "the truth of Christianity" and "matters of theology." They lament the decay of intellectual attainments and of intellectual interests among the clergy and the weakening of their influence in the universities. They lament also the indisposition to take orders on the part of able men whose spiritual aims fit them for office in the Church. But they do not face the question whether these results may not be due, in part at least, to the fact that the clergy are expected to give assent not merely to " the truth of Christianity," but also to certain "matters of theology " contained in the creeds and articles which theologians and politicians from the second century to the sixteenth have formulated as the faith of the Church. They speak as if the whole body of Church doctrine were so organically united that it must be accepted or rejected *en bloc*. Yet they have themselves pointed out that Christian theo-

[1] *Report of the Archbishops' First Committee*, p. 9.

logy was affected at each critical stage of its growth
by the current philosophy of the day. It adopted
not only the language, but also the mode of thought,
at one period of the Alexandrian school, at
another period of Aristotle[1].

To the student of science and philosophy also
these schools serve as an inspiration. But he can
prove himself worthy to enter into their labours
only if he has complete freedom to revise their
results in the light of wider experience and inde-
pendent reflexion. In thought as in life growth
implies both selection and rejection. Is the
thought of the Church to stand aloof from this
law? Is it to be bound for ever to the formulae
devised by its leaders when philosophy was less
complex, when science was in its infancy, and when
modern historical methods were as yet undreamed
of? In this matter the Church of England is at
the cross-roads. It may hold to its traditions and
maintain a system of doctrine which is out of
touch with the results of the intellect in other
departments. Or, on the other hand, it may have
faith in the unity of truth and courage to prove
all things—even old traditions—and to hold fast

[1] *Report*, pp. 19, 20.

only that which is good. The Church is not being called upon to discard the doctrines in which men of old expressed their faith. Perhaps the time is not yet ripe for formulating beliefs. But it may well be asked to revise its attitude to them and to discriminate between their historical and their present significance. Perhaps it will also listen to the modest plea of an Army Chaplain that the consciences of the clergy should be relieved from what he calls "the insincerity of being concerned with the Thirty-nine Articles[1]." Courage is needed to face these questions; but, if they are faced with courage, then we may look forward to the day when the prophecy will be fulfilled and the Church shall again be called the City of Truth[2], the inspirer and guardian of all man's spiritual interests.

The same problem concerns us as a College. By our Statutes we form a House dedicated to education, religion, learning, and research. Time was in our history when all these interests might be served by each of the fellows. But the field has grown in extent, and every part of it needs more

---

[1] N. S. Talbot, *The Church in the Furnace*, p. 287.
[2] Zech. viii. 3.

intensive culture; and each of us, absorbed in his
own special work, is apt to become indifferent to
that of his neighbour. The specialisation is
necessary; but it has manifest drawbacks even in
a purely intellectual regard. We need to be
constantly reminded of the unity of spirit which
animates, or should animate, every branch of
academic work, and of the unity of the object
which it seeks. All alike are in quest of truth;
and the only atmosphere in which this quest can
live is freedom—freedom of enquiry, freedom of
belief, freedom of teaching. If the theologian is
in fetters from which the man of science and the
philosopher are free, this unity of spirit is lost.
But if the Archbishops' Committee are right and
this same atmosphere of freedom is "essential to
sound theological development[1]," then the intellectual and the religious life of the College may be
animated by a common spirit.

And not in spirit only but also in the object of
their quest there is a profound unity beneath all
superficial differences. However narrow may be
the sphere of any one man's intellectual labours,
he is working on the structure of the great fane

[1] *Report*, p. 21.

of Truth, and he may be inspired by a vision of the fabric of which he is a builder. In the southwestern corner of this Chapel, on one of the Tudor roses which decorate it, there may be seen, in the centre of the flower and in place of the stamens, a sculptured image of the Virgin. The nameless workman who executed it had been told off to carve a rose; and he did so. But his eyes caught a glimpse of the higher vision which he was helping to shape in stone; and under his hands the emblem of the Tudors became a symbol of our Lady in whose honour the Chapel was founded. Which thing is an allegory. From the most concentrated devotion to a minute problem, it is right and necessary that the mind should rise sometimes to the wider view and see the particular subject in the light of the whole system. This much the intellect needs for its own sake. But no man is saved by the intellect alone, nor can the man of intellect stand in isolation from his fellows. He who has escaped out of the cave of ignorance and false opinion into the light of the sun feels the duty laid upon him of guiding others on the way he came. For this reason education is combined with learning and research in the vocation of the scholar. He should be a giver as well as a getter. Knowledge alone cannot emancipate the spirit of man until it is freed from the taint of selfishness and united with the spirit of love, which is the spirit of Christ.

We stand in the valley of decision, and, according as we turn to one hand or the other, the future will be affected for generations to come. On the one hand the prospect before us is a battle of conflicting interests—of nation against nation, of class against class, of religion against knowledge. On the other hand is the vision of diverse activities united by a common spirit and pressing towards the same goal. Who has eyes to discern the vision and power to bring it into being? To those who went out from among us at their country's call, not counting their lives dear in the service of so great a cause—to them we have looked to build a better England. Faithful unto death, many of them return no more. But those whom God has spared to come back to us bring with them an experience of reality wedded to the ideals and energy of youth; while others, too young as yet to grasp the sword, have lived in the light of a great example and have learned that love is better than life. Through their labours I see arise a mighty nation, its spirit purified by fiery trials, the home of ordered freedom and a surety for the world's peace, with renewed strength pressing towards the mark for the prize of its high calling. I see a living Church, loyal to the gospel of the Master whose life was the light of men, no longer suspicious of the free course of knowledge, but itself the inspirer of all things pure and lofty. And I see a great College, the servant of God and of the people, yet knowing no master in its loyalty to truth, penetrating into the secrets of nature and of mind, mindful alike of the unity of knowledge and of its human worth, and year by year sending forth its sons to be leaders in thought and in action throughout the world. Is it an unsubstantial vision? "When the Lord turned again the captivity of Zion, we were like them that dream." But such dreams have a way of making themselves true.

And now the time returns again:
  Our souls exult: and London's towers
Receive the Lamb of God to dwell
  In England's green and pleasant bowers.

www.ingramcontent.com/pod-product-compliance
Ingram Content Group UK Ltd.
Pitfield, Milton Keynes, MK11 3LW, UK
UKHW042148280225
455719UK00001B/198

9 781107 629264